Key terms

Use Chapter 10 of your textbook to match the heads and tails to define the

Heads	Tails
Economic boom	One of the two main political parties in the USA – bro... ....conservative with a belief in minimal government intervention, low taxes and isolationism
Laissez-faire	Taxes on imported goods which make them more expensive
Republican Party	A period of economic prosperity characterised by increased trade, higher share prices, bigger profits and higher wages
Democratic Party	The belief that one race is superior to others
Tariffs	The system of producing goods in factories on assembly lines, resulting in faster production and cheaper prices
Federal system	A system whereby individual states look after their own internal affairs (state government) and the government in Washington DC (federal government) deals with foreign affairs, taxation policy and matters of national security
Mass production	The movement of foreign people into another country
Red Scare	The belief that government should stay out of the affairs of the individual and business
Immigration	The banning of the sale and production of alcohol
Ku Klux Klan	One of the two main political parties in the USA – broadly liberal with a belief in limited government intervention to help the poorest in society
Racism	Religious followers who believe in the literal truth of their holy book, e.g. the Bible
Prohibition	Secret racist and white supremacist organisation in the USA
Fundamentalist	Fear of communism spreading to the USA
Speculation	A period of economic downturn characterised by decreased trade, higher unemployment and falling share prices
Depression	The head of the government and head of state in the USA
Hundred Days	Buying and selling shares on the stock market to try to make a profit
Alphabet agencies	The legal framework of a nation that sets out rules on how government is elected, the powers of each branch of government and citizens' rights
Congress	The parliament of the USA that passes new laws
President	The highest court in the USA that checks the power of the President and Congress – it can declare laws or actions by the President unconstitutional
Supreme Court	Government agencies set up to deal with the Depression
US Constitution	Literally the first hundred days for a new president where he sets out new legislation

1 Key Question 1: How far did the US economy boom in the 1920s?

• Causes and features of the economic boom (pages 298–303)

1 Use the information in the text boxes below to complete the diagram to summarise the causes of the economic boom. Draw a small sketch next to each factor to illustrate.

The USA had lots of raw materials such as oil, coal and iron ore.	Low taxes led to higher profits for companies and higher wages.	Assembly lines produced new consumer goods like cars and radios.	US agriculture was the most efficient and productive in the world.
The USA had given war loans to the Allies that had to be repaid.	Advertising on billboards and on radios helped sell new products.	Hire purchase schemes allowed people to buy products on credit.	Electricity was more available as well as new inventions like rayon.
The government put tariffs on foreign goods to protect US businesses.	Confidence was high, leading to greater investment in companies.	Banks lent money to people to buy shares 'on the margin'.	US trade prospered from weapons, munitions and food sold to the Allies.

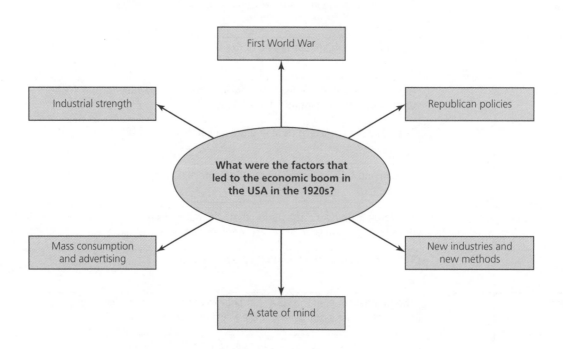

2 Use the table below to explain how each factor helped cause an economic boom. Add an example in the middle column from the diagram in question 1. An example has been done for you.

Factor that led to the 'boom'	Example	How did this cause an economic boom in the USA in the 1920s?
US industrial strength	The USA had lots of raw materials such as oil, coal and iron ore.	This would help cause the economic boom because it meant that US industries had easy and cheap access to raw materials, which would lead to cheaper costs, cheaper prices and therefore higher profits.
First World War		
New industries and new methods		
Mass consumption and advertising		
Republican policies		
A state of mind		

Industrial strength (page 299)

3 Study page 299 then answer the following questions.

a What was the population of the USA by 1923? Where did most people live by this point?

....

....

b Why was a higher urban population important for the economic boom?

....

....

c Study Figure 1. What raw materials did the USA have plenty of?

....

....

d How did these raw materials help fuel an economic boom in the 1920s?

....

e Where were the most densely populated areas of the USA?

....

....

f Why would a well-established textile industry such as cotton benefit American industry?

....

....

g Why do you think that overproduction in agriculture could cause a problem for farmers?

....

....

....

The impact of war (page 300)

4 Study page 300 then answer the following questions.

a How did the First World War benefit the USA?

....

....

b How did involvement in the First World War affect the chemical industry in the USA?

....

....

c How did the First World War impact the aviation (aircraft) industry?

....

....

d How did the First World War help and hinder the USA's 'second industrial revolution'? Use the text boxes provided to complete the table below.

Farmers sold foodstuffs to the Allies leading to overproduction at the end of the war.	The USA took over European trade during the war, forming new markets for US goods.	Arms sales to Europe led to industrial growth and massive profits to invest.
US banks gave war loans to the Allies which had to be paid back with interest.	There was a minor depression from 1920 to 1921 as US industry readjusted to peacetime.	New industries grew in the USA such as chemicals, explosives and later plastics.

Helped	Hindered

Republican policies (page 300)

5 Study page 300. How did the policies of the Republican presidents help cause the economic boom in the USA in the 1920s? Link together the heads and tails in the table below by drawing a line.

Heads (policies)	Tails (explanation)
Laissez-faire	This would help cause the economic boom because it meant foreign goods were more expensive so people in the USA would buy American, leading to greater profits.
Rugged individualism	This would help cause the economic boom because it meant business was left alone to expand and make profits without government regulations increasing their costs.
Low taxation	This would help cause the economic boom because it allowed the 'captains of industry' (e.g. steel and oil) to control a vital sector of industry and make huge profits leading to an increase in share prices.
Tariffs	This would help cause the economic boom because people were expected to solve their own problems, which would decrease government spending and promote business.
Trusts	This would help cause the economic boom because it allowed businesses to make higher profits, pay higher wages and allowed people to spend more of their income on new goods.

The car and mass production (pages 301–302)

6 Read the information and study the sources on pages 301–302 of your textbook then complete the tasks below.

a Who revolutionised the automobile industry in the USA?

....

b Briefly describe how this system of mass production worked.

....

....

....

c Study the diagram below which shows the knock-on effects of the automobile industry on the US economy, then answer the questions that follow.

i What other industries benefited from the automobile industry in the USA?

....

....

ii Describe how the automobile industry led to the creation of more jobs.

....

....

....

iii What industry was the single biggest employer in the USA in the 1920s?

....

iv How did the motor car help increase the size of cities in the 1920s?

....

....

Mass consumption and confidence (page 303)

7 Read the information and sources on page 303 of your textbook then complete the tasks below.

a Study Figure 5 on page 303 of your textbook. Complete the four bar charts below using the information in the source.

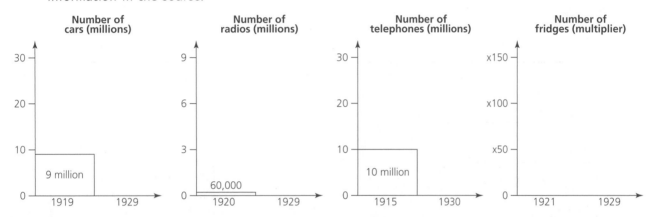

b Use the text boxes provided to complete the table below. In the last column, explain how each new method of marketing would have helped lead to an economic boom.

| Billboards and posters were used so new products could be seen from cars. | People in remote areas had access to new products. | Radio adverts played at home and in cars between music. | Banks were willing to lend and companies let people 'buy now, pay later'. |

| Nearly one-third of Americans bought goods from catalogues in 1928. | Eight out of ten radios and six out of ten cars were bought on credit. | New chains of stores sprung up in the 1920s, such as Woolworths. | The same products were now available nationwide. |

Marketing technique	Examples	How would this have helped lead to an economic boom?
Advertising		
Mail-order companies		
Hire-purchase schemes		
Chain stores		

c   How had attitudes towards spending changed among many Americans by the 1920s?

....

....

....

d   How did high confidence affect the behaviour of the following groups? Link the groups in the centre with the details in the text boxes by drawing a line.

They had confidence to spend their income on leisure activities.

They had the confidence to invest in new technology.

They had confidence to allow Americans to buy shares 'on the margin'.

Business

They had confidence to increase consumer lending.

Banks

They had confidence to buy new products on credit–hire purchase.

Ordinary Americans

They had the confidence to buy shares on the stock market.

They had confidence to give loans to help companies expand.

They had confidence to set up new companies.

e   Explain how high confidence was vital to the economic boom. Include the following words in your answer: *loans; shares; credit; investment; income.*

....

....

....

....

....

• Economic problems in the 1920s (pages 304–306)

Agriculture (page 304)

8 Read the information and study the source on page 304 of your textbook then complete the following tasks.

a What evidence is there that farmers were not benefiting from the economic boom in the USA in the 1920s?

....

b Study Source 6 on page 304 of your textbook. Draw lines to link the source details with their meanings in the table below.

Source detail	Meaning
The factory smoke with the dollar sign	This suggests that the farmer cannot afford to run his farm anymore or has too many debts.
The farmer looking out to the factories	This suggests that agriculture loses out while industry booms.
The 'FARM FOR SALE' sign	This suggests that industry in the cities is making huge profits.

c Why were farmers facing economic hardship in the 1920s? Use the key provided to colour code the text boxes below.

> **Declining exports** ☐   **New competitors** ☐   **Overproduction** ☐   **Falling prices** ☐

Canadian wheat producers were even more efficient.	The US population was declining so there were fewer mouths to feed.	In 1921, farm prices fell by 50 per cent for cereals compared to 1919.
US tariffs meant Europe responded by putting tariffs on US foodstuffs.	New machinery and fertilisers led to surplus food that wouldn't sell.	Lack of income caused farms to go bankrupt due to debt.

> The First World War had led to more efficient farming techniques.
>
> The end of the war meant less demand for food in Europe.

d How many Americans lived in rural areas of the USA in the early 1920s?

....

e Briefly describe how some farmers still prospered during the 1920s. Add some examples to your description.

....

....

....

f   Why were African Americans among the worst affected by problems in farming?

....

....

....

g   What were the consequences of the problems in farming for the rural population?

....

....

Traditional industries (pages 305–306)

9   Read the information on pages 305–306 of your textbook then complete the tasks below.

a   What percentage of the population was estimated to be living below the 'poverty line' in the 1920s? What wage per week was considered the poverty line?

....

b   What problems did workers in traditional industries face during the 1920s? Use the text boxes below to complete the table.

Too much was being produced, leading to low prices and low profits.	Electricity-generating technology was more efficient at producing energy.	Skilled workers like shoe-makers couldn't compete against mechanisation.	Domestic boilers in homes were more efficient and needed less fuel.
Many manufacturers were switching to electricity or oil to power their factories.	Leather and cotton industries could not sell their products overseas due to tariffs.	Pay rises never matched the dividends of shareholders and company profits.	New man-made materials like rayon were cheaper and more popular.

Coal industry	Textile industry

c Study Source 9 on page 305 of your textbook. Why was the Republican government unlikely to help these hunger marchers? Explain your answer.

....

....

....

d Why did the growth in industry in the 1920s not produce many jobs in the USA?

....

....

e What percentage of the population in the USA remained unemployed from 1920 to 1929?

....

10 Read Source 10 on page 306. Was Herbert Hoover right? Use the text boxes provided and the diagram below to decide which groups in the USA prospered from the economic boom and which groups did not. The more you think they prospered the closer to the top you need to place them. The less they prospered the closer to the bottom you need to place them. Add a short explanation next to each one, justifying your decisions.

Coal miner	Black American farmer	Automobile worker
Orange farmer	Radio factory owner	Middle-class investor

Winners

Losers

Key Question 2: How far did US society change in the 1920s?

• The Roaring Twenties (pages 307–309)

1 Read the information and study the sources on pages 307–309 of your textbook then complete the tasks below.

a Study Figure 2 on page 307. How were population patterns changing in the USA?

....

....

....

....

b What were the 'Roaring Twenties'? Write a ROARING mnemonic to describe different aspects of the 'Roaring Twenties' in the USA. Make sure you include the following: *radio; jazz music; sport; cinema; the car; changing morals; leisure time.*

> R
>
> O
>
> **A**lmost everyone is the USA was listening to the new radios in their homes as a family and in their cars
>
> R
>
> I
>
> N
>
> G

c Study Source 3 on page 308. What does this source suggest about the attitudes of conservative Americans towards entertainment? Use source details to explain.

....

....

....

d How did Hollywood respond to conservative opinions on lowering morals in cinema?

....

....

e How far did changing morals affect actual sexual behaviour?

....

....

• Women in the 1920s (pages 310–311)

2 Read the information and study all of the sources on pages 310–311 of your textbook then complete the following tasks.

a Complete the diagram below to describe what was expected of women before the First World War. Make sure you mention middle-class and working-class women in your descriptions.

> **Women in the USA before the First World War**

b Complete this table summarising changes in the 1920s.

Factor affecting attitudes towards women's roles	Why this factor caused a change in attitudes and women's roles in 1920s, USA
Impact of the First World War	
The vote	
The motor car	
Housework	

c Study Source 8 on page 311. How did the lives of rural women differ from those in urban areas?

....

....

....

d How far did opportunities for women improve in the 1920s? Use pages 310–311 to complete the table below. Write a conclusion in the space provided underneath the table.

Factor	Women's opportunities had improved...	Women's opportunities were still limited...
Political life		
Employment		
Home, family and marriage		
Social freedoms		

Overall, the lives of women had/had not improved in the USA in the 1920s because ....

....

....

This was due to the fact ....

....

....

• Intolerance in the 1920s (pages 312–319)

3 Read the text boxes below and colour code them using the key provided to categorise the different causes of intolerance in the USA in the 1920s.

Racial intolerance ☐	Religious intolerance ☐	Political intolerance ☐

'Jim Crow' laws were passed to segregate black Americans in the South.	In 1919, 400,000 workers around the USA went on strike.	By 1917, Asian immigration had been halted.
The 'Bible Belt' had many fundamentalist Protestant churches.	The USA was mainly Protestant and feared Jewish immigration.	City workers feared losing their jobs to foreigners.
The KKK was a popular white supremacist movement in the 1920s.	Many eastern and southern European immigrants were Catholic.	The 1917 Russian Revolution caused a fear of communist immigrants.
Anarchists spread the idea of overthrowing the government.	Special boarding schools tried to destroy Native American culture.	There was a strong anti-German feeling after the First World War.

Immigration and the Red Scare (pages 312–314)

4 Study Figure 10 on page 312. Why might the figures in this source have helped contribute towards increased intolerance in the 1920s? Use source details to explain your answer.

....

....

....

....

5 Study Figure 11 then answer the following questions.

a Which ethnic group made up the highest percentage of the US immigrant population in the early twentieth century?

....

....

b What was the total number of white and white Europeans in the US immigrant population (including Russians)?

....

....

c What was the total number of non-European immigrants as part of the US population?

....

....

d Does this graph prove that the USA was a 'melting pot'? Explain your answer.

....

....

6 Use the information and sources on pages 312–314 of your textbook to complete the tasks below.

a Study Source 12. What do the words of US Attorney General, Mitchell Palmer, suggest about American fears in the 1920s? Use source details to explain your answer.

....

....

....

b What was meant by the term 'Red Scare'?

....

....

....

c What evidence was there to prove the 'Red Scare' was a genuine threat in the USA?

....

....

....

d How did Mitchell Palmer and J. Edgar Hoover contribute to the fear of a communist revolution in the USA?

....

....

....

e Read the section on Sacco and Vanzetti on page 314 of your textbook. Explain why their trial is seen as a mistrial.

....

....

....

The experience of African Americans (pages 314–316)

7 Use the information and sources on pages 314–316 of your textbook to complete the tasks below.

a How had the first black Americans arrived in the USA?

....

b Give two reasons why white governments in the Southern USA introduced laws to segregate black Americans.

   i ....

   ....

   ii ....

   ....

c List three ways that segregation laws (Jim Crow Laws) legally separated white and black Americans.

   i ....

   ii ....

   iii ....

d Examine the Factfile on the Ku Klux Klan on page 315 of your textbook. Use the information to complete the diagram below.

Origins of the KKK	Aims of the KKK

KKK

Methods of the KKK	Rise and decline of the KKK

e Study Source 16 on page 315 of your textbook. What does this photo suggest about racism in the USA in the 1920s?

....

....

....

....

f What was lynching?

....

....

g How did many black Americans respond to the racism in the Southern states of the USA?

....

....

h Compare the quality of life for black Americans in the South and North of the USA by using the text boxes to complete the table.

Better job and education opportunities	Jim Crow laws segregated everyday life, e.g. toilets, schools	KKK violence: thousands of African Americans were whipped and lynched
African Americans were denied the right to vote in many states	A growing black middle class in cities like New York	Most African Americans were 'sharecroppers' on white-owned farms
Many rural conservatives still had racist beliefs stemming from slavery	Marcus Garvey urged black Americans to be proud of their culture	Jazz music gave fame to some African Americans such as Louis Armstrong
In Harlem, New York, a 'renaissance' flourished – poets, artists and singers	The National Association for the Advancement of Black People (NAACP)	African Americans could enter politics more freely

North	South

i Was the NAACP a successful political organisation? Explain your answer.

....

....

....

....

j Write a short description of the problems black people might encounter living in Chicago in the 1920s. Include the following in your entry: *life expectancy; poverty; housing; quality of life; racial prejudice.*

> **Life in the North**
>
> ....
>
> ....
>
> ....
>
> ....
>
> ....
>
> ....

The Monkey Trial (page 319)

8 Read the information and study the source on page 319 of your textbook then complete the tasks below.

a Draw lines to link the two theories in the centre with the correct statements.

	Written by biologist Charles Darwin in his 1859 book *Origin of the Species*	
Evolutionists wanted Darwin's theory taught in science lessons	**Theory of evolution**	Believed by a majority of urban Americans by the 1920s
Believed mainly by rural Protestants in the 'Bible Belt' states like Tennessee	**Creationist theory**	Based on a literal belief in the creation story in the Old Testament of the Bible
	Christian fundamentalists wanted creationism taught in schools, not evolution	

b Why could the Monkey Trial be considered a victory for the evolutionists?

....

....

c Study Source 21 on page 319 of your textbook then answer the following questions.

    i What evidence is there in the source that Bryan is being ridiculed for his beliefs?

    ....

    ii What evidence is there in the source that Bryan was intolerant of other points of view?

    ....

• Prohibition (pages 320–324)

9 Read the information and study the sources on page 320 of your textbook then complete the tasks below.

    a What were the names of the two main temperance movements by the end of the nineteenth century?

      i ....

      ii ....

    b Which type of American citizen was most likely to support the temperance movements and their call for Prohibition in the USA?

    ....

    ....

    ....

    c Why was Prohibition introduced in 1920? Use the key provided to colour code the different reasons in the text boxes.

Historical ☐	Socio-economic ☐	Political ☐	Religious or moral ☐
Leading industrialists believed workers would be more productive.	Politicians believed supporting the dries would win them votes.	Alcohol was believed to lead to lawlessness and crime.
Some campaigners linked drink to Russian communism.	Temperance movements had been campaigning since the nineteenth century.	By 1916, 21 states had already banned saloons.
Dries claimed that sober workers would take less time off work.	The Church claimed that alcohol was the cause of society's evils.	Alcohol abuse was thought to cause misery to children and families.
Many big breweries were run by German immigrants.	Drunken behaviour was a major cause of disease, including STIs.	Some rural states had already got Prohibition laws.

d What was meant by the terms 'wets' and 'dries'?

....

....

e What were the terms of the Volstead Act?

....

....

10 Read the information and study all of the sources on pages 321–324 of your textbook then complete the tasks below.

a What year was Prohibition introduced? ....

b What year did Prohibition end? ....

c Define the following terms:

• bootleg liquor ....

• speakeasy ....

• bootlegger ....

d Why did Prohibition fail? Use the text boxes below to complete the table opposite. In the last column, write a short explanation of why that factor would lead to the failure of Prohibition.

Prohibition agents were poorly paid and there were too few to enforce the law.	By 1925 there were more speakeasies than there had been saloons in 1919.	Enforcement was made impossible by the fact that millions ignored the law.
The gangster Al Capone made $60 million a year from speakeasies.	Illegal stills provided moonshine to meet demand for alcohol.	Bootleggers supplied illegal booze from Canada and from across the sea.
Local officials were bribed by breweries and bootleggers.	Gangsters were ruthless and murdered opponents, e.g. St Valentine's Day Massacre.	Senior officers and judges were often bribed, which meant it was difficult to convict criminals.
Agents couldn't locate hidden speakeasies or patrol borders effectively.	Al Capone was popular in Chicago – he gave generous tips and was charitable.	Government officials and senior police officers were involved in the liquor trade.

Reason for failure	Evidence	Why would this cause Prohibition to fail?
Demand		
Enforcement		
Corruption		
Organised crime		

e Explain how corruption made enforcement of Prohibition difficult.

....

....

....

f Study Source 30 on page 322. What is meant by the caption 'The National Gesture'? Use source details to explain your answer.

....

....

....

g Why did Prohibition allow gangsters to flourish? Try to list three reasons.

....

....

....

h Why did gangsterism help lead to the ending of Prohibition? Try to list three reasons.

....

....

....

....

11 Use your answers from questions 9–10 and the information and sources on pages 320–324 to answer the following question: How far does Prohibition deserve the title 'The Noble Experiment'? Explain your answer in the spaces below.

Prohibition does/does not deserves the title 'The Noble Experiment' because ....

....

....

This view can be supported by the fact that ....

....

Furthermore, ...

....

Key Question 3: What were the causes and consequences of the Wall Street Crash?

• Speculation and the stock market (pages 325–326)

1 Read the information and study the sources on pages 325–326 of your textbook then complete the tasks below.

a How does investment and the stock market work? Use the flow diagram below to summarise the information on page 325 in the Factfile titled 'Investment and the stock market'. Use the headings in the flow diagram to help you.

1. Investors and shareholders	→	2. Shareholders' returns	→	3. Share prices	→	4. New York stock market (Wall Street)

b Briefly explain why share prices continued to rise through much of the 1920s.

....

....

c How many share owners were there in:

i 1920: ....

ii 1929: ....

d Why can speculators be considered 'gamblers'?

....

....

....

e What was 'buying on the margin'?

....

....

f   Which year saw the highest rises in share prices in the USA?

....

g   Below is a simple diagram describing how high confidence causes share prices to rise. Underneath, draw your own version of the diagram to show how low confidence could cause share prices to fall.

2   Use the information and sources on pages 325–327 of your textbook to complete the tasks below.

a   Which two industries in the USA had already begun to decline by the mid-1920s?

....

b   What signs were there in other industries that the economy was starting to decline by 1929?

....

....

....

c   How did tariffs add to the economic problems faced by US companies?

....

....

....

d What factor caused many shareholders to lose confidence by the summer of 1929?

....

....

e Use the text boxes below to complete the timeline of the Wall Street Crash in 1929.

1929 June Sept Oct **CRASH**	Factory production and steel production start to decline Last day of rising share prices 'Black Tuesday' – panic selling of 13 million shares on the US stock market Index loses 43 points and banks stop supporting stock market 'Black Thursday' – big drop in share prices – banks buy stock to stabilise markets Market recovers from initial drop in share prices Ticker machines break due to selling – many don't know if they are ruined 'Babson Break' – economist Roger Babson predicts a crash in the near future

f What were the causes of the Wall Street Crash? Use the text boxes below to complete the table overleaf. In the last column, you need to add a 'blame' rating and justify it with a brief explanation. One has been done for you.

The car industry was producing more cars than it could sell by 1929.	People bought shares believing that prices would never stop rising.	Europe had put up its own tariffs in response to US tariffs.	Companies spent $3 billion on advertising to sell surplus goods.
Banks lent money to people to buy shares 'on the margin' causing debt.	Banks refused to support share prices when panic selling took hold.	Speculation was a gamble and pushed prices higher than they were worth.	American businesses could not sell surplus goods to overseas markets.

Cause of Crash	Evidence	'Blame' rating /10 Explanation
Distribution of income	Over 50 per cent of the US population lived below the poverty line. Farmers and those in traditional industries like textiles were already poor.	Blame rating: .... This would help cause the Crash because it meant that lots of poor Americans couldn't buy the new goods, even on credit. This would lead to less sales once the wealthier Americans had bought them, with many having to pay back loans and interest.
Overproduction		Blame rating: ....
Over-speculation		Blame rating: ....
Tariffs		Blame rating: ....
Banks		Blame rating: ....

• From Crash to Depression (pages 327–329)

3 Read the information and study the sources on pages 327–329 of your textbook then complete the following tasks.

a Study the diagram below. Write no more than 50 words to describe how the Wall Street Crash caused a depression in the USA.

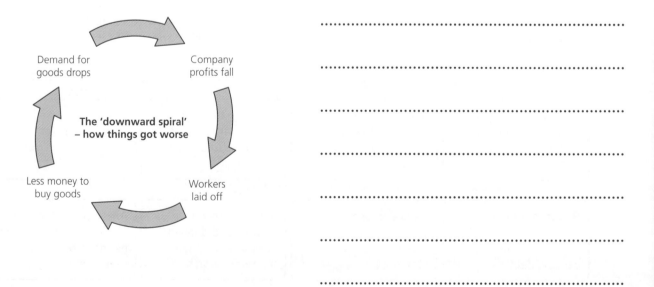

....

....

....

....

....

....

b Name two groups of Americans who lost the most in the Wall Street Crash and explain how it affected them.

....

....

....

....

c What were the economic consequences of the Wall Street Crash? Complete the diagram below by adding the information in the text boxes then drawing a small sketch to illustrate. If you think any of the consequences link, draw a line to show this on the diagram.

In 1929, 659 banks went bankrupt; in 1930, 1352 more failed; by 1933, 5000.	Lenders were less willing to give loans to businesses or mortgages for homes.	Business profits fell drastically and share prices dropped further.	Spending on consumer goods dropped so factories reduced output.
By 1933 there were 14 million unemployed as companies laid off workers.	Farmers' wealth dropped to just $5 billion by 1933.	Industrial and farm output was cut by 40 per cent between 1928 and 1933.	People withdrew their savings – over $1 billion by 1931.

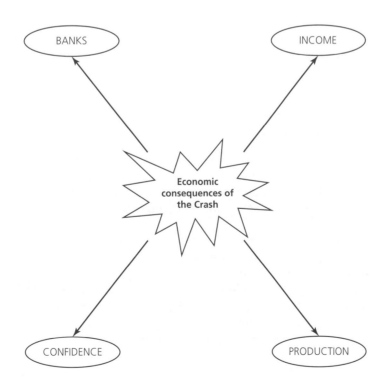

• The impact of the Depression (pages 330–331)

4 Read the information and study the sources on pages 330–331 of your textbook then complete the tasks below.

a Which group in the USA was hardest hit by the Depression?

....

b Study Source 6 on page 330. Use the information and the source to briefly describe the 'dustbowl' and how it made the effects of the Depression even worse for many Americans.

....

....

....

....

c What was meant by the term 'Hooverville'?

....

....

d Use the key provided to colour code the different social consequences of the Wall Street Crash on rural and urban areas of the USA.

> **Rural Americans** ☐   **Urban Americans** ☐

Wheat and fruit were left to rot and animals were killed.	Farms were repossessed by banks. Many farmers resisted.	Shanty towns became a normal sight for the homeless.	Black agricultural labourers were often hardest hit.
In 1932, 50 per cent of workers in Cleveland were unemployed.	An estimated 2 million workers travelled by rail searching for work.	Malnutrition and starvation were more commonplace.	Bread lines were a common sight in most cities.

• The 1932 presidential election (pages 332–333)

5 Read the information and study the sources on pages 332–333 of your textbook then complete the tasks below.

a What year was the presidential election between Hoover and Roosevelt?

....

b Hoover was regarded as a 'do-nothing' president. Use the text boxes below to complete the table to decide how far this statement is true.

Hoover set up a Farm Board to try to keep food prices up.	Hoover insisted prosperity was 'just around the corner'.	The Reconstruction Finance Company tried to prop up banks.	Republicans were against government help – laissez-faire.	Hoover blocked government aid to create jobs in 1932.

Hoover believed relief should be provided by charities or the states.	Hoover introduced more tax cuts in 1930 and 1931 to stimulate spending.	Invested in public works programmes like the Hoover Dam.	Hoover introduced tariffs to try to protect US industry.

'Do nothing'	'Do something'

c Explain why you think Hoover's tactics in dealing with the Bonus Marchers would have damaged his chances of re-election in 1932.

....

....

....

....

d What characteristics of Franklin D. Roosevelt helped his victory in 1932? Summarise using the headings below and the information on pages 332–333.

His political experience: ....

....

....

His beliefs: ....

....

....

His plans: ....

....

....

e Study Source 15 on page 333. Choose three quotes from the speech that you think would have inspired Americans to vote for Roosevelt.

i ....

ii ....

ii ....

f What strategies did Roosevelt use to spread his political message across the USA?

....

....

....

g What were the election results in 1932?

....

....

h Why did Roosevelt win the 1932 election? Use your answers to the questions on Key Question 3 and the information on pages 327–333 to add explanations in the table below. Make a judgement in the space underneath the table to explain which factor you think was the most important.

Factor	Examples	Explanation
Depression	• Fourteen million unemployed by 1932 • Farmers lost their land • Bank closures • Poverty, homelessness and hunger in the cities • Hoovervilles and bread lines	
Republican policies	• Laissez-faire – very little government intervention • Rugged individualism – Republicans believed charities and state governments should act, not federal government	
Hoover's actions	• Public works schemes had limited impact on unemployment • Blocked $1.2 billion in Congressional aid to create jobs • Introduced more tariffs • Government reaction to Bonus Marchers	
F.D. Roosevelt	• Good public speaker and believed in American Dream • Promised a New Deal for the American people • Proposed government help for those affected by the Depression • Political experience	

The most important factor for Roosevelt's election in 1932 was ....

This was because ....

....

....

For example, ...

....

....

4 Key Question 4: How successful was the New Deal?

• The Hundred Days (pages 334–336)

1 Read the information and study the sources on pages 334–336 of your textbook then complete the tasks below.

a What were the 'Hundred Days'?

....

....

b What was the 'Brains Trust'?

....

....

c Study Source 1 on page 334. What does this source suggest as the main aim of Roosevelt's New Deal legislation? Use source details to explain your answer.

....

....

....

....

d Why do you think Roosevelt's first priority was banking?

....

....

....

e What were Roosevelt's 'fireside chats'? How many Americans listened to these?

....

....

f Roosevelt's aims are often summed up as the 'Three Rs'. Link together the 'Three Rs' on the left with their aims on the right by drawing a line.

Three Rs	Aims
Relief	Revive the economy and get people back to work and stimulate businesses
Recovery	Pass new laws to make the USA a better place for ordinary Americans
Reform	Help relieve the poverty of those worst hit by the effects of the Depression

g Briefly describe how Roosevelt tackled the banking crisis in the USA.

   i Emergency Banking Act

   ....

   ....

   ii Securities Exchange Commission

   ....

   ....

h Study Source 2 on page 334. Does this source suggest that Roosevelt's actions to tackle the banking crisis were successful or not? Explain your answer.

....

....

....

....

i How many proposals did Roosevelt send to Congress in the first Hundred Days? How many of these were adopted by Congress?

....

....

....

j Use the text boxes below to complete the table provided to explain the aims and impact of Roosevelt's first Hundred Days legislation. The last column requires you to give an explanation. Some text boxes can be used more than once. One has been done for you.

| Unemployed | The poor | Business/industry | Farmers | Banks |

| All banks had to close; 5000 trustworthy ones reopened. | Set out fair wages and improved work conditions. | Young men could sign up for six months of conservation work. | New rules and regulations to stop reckless speculation. | Set quotas on production to force prices upwards. |

| Public money was used to build schools, roads, dams, bridges and airports. | Built dams to irrigate land, provide jobs and electricity to homes. | Around 2.5 million men were helped – many worked in national parks. | $500 million was spent on soup kitchens and employment schemes. | Helped farms modernise methods. Some got help with debt. |

New Deal legislation/ agencies	Who was this aimed at helping?	Evidence	How would this help during the Depression?
Emergency Banking Act	Banks	All banks had to close; 5000 trustworthy ones reopened.	This would help restore confidence in the banks and encourage people to save again. With more savings, banks could lend money.
Securities Exchange Commission			
Federal Emergency Relief Administration (FERA)			
Civilian Conservation Corps (CCC)			
Agricultural Adjustment Administration (AAA)			
Public Works Administration (PWA)			
National Recovery Administration (NRA)			
Tennessee Valley Authority (TVA)			

k Examine the different agencies in the table above. Why do you think they were often referred to as alphabet agencies?

....

....

l Study Source 3 on page 335 of your textbook. Draw lines to match up the source details to the correct meaning in the table below.

Source 3A	
The man with FDR on his waistcoat	This suggests that the man is Herbert Hoover, the former US president who was blamed for his lack of action during the early years of the Depression.
The rubbish bin with a sign saying 'Prosperity is around the corner'	This suggests that the man is Roosevelt, the new US president from 1933.
The man walking off with H.H. written on his briefcase	This suggests the old Republican policies and promises are being thrown out by the Democrats.

Source 3B	
Uncle Sam – the bearded man in the middle hugging the other men – 'Employee' and 'Employer'	This suggests that joining the NRA was the patriotic thing to do – the bald eagle was the national symbol of the USA.
The NRA badges with the eagle symbol on them – they were blue in colour	This suggests that workers and business were working together with the US government.

m Study Figure 4 and the text on page 335 of your textbook then answer the questions below.

i Which seven states did the TVA cut across?

....

....

ii How many dams did the TVA build across the seven states?

....

iii Which major river were many of these dams built across?

....

iv How do you think these dams would help the economies of these states?

....

....

....

n Why did Roosevelt target the Tennessee Valley in his Hundred Days reforms?

....

....

....

o Read Sources 5, 6 and 7 and the Factfile on page 336. Complete the diagram below to give details of the success of the New Deal introduced as part of Roosevelt's first Hundred Days.

What successes were there in the First New Deal?

• The Second New Deal (page 337)

2 Read the information and study the sources on pages 337 of your textbook then complete the tasks below.

a How was the focus of the Second New Deal different from the New Deal legislation set out in Roosevelt's first Hundred Days?

....

....

....

b Use the text boxes below to complete the table provided to explain the aims and impact of Roosevelt's Second New Deal. The last column requires you to give an explanation. Some can be used more than once.

| Unemployed | Workers | Elderly/sick/widows | Farmers |

| Business had to allow trade unions to negotiate pay and conditions | This brought together all job creation agencies into one | Helped over half a million poor farmers move to better land | Created jobs for office workers, artists, actors and photographers | Set up unemployment insurance – workers and employers contributed |

| Federal and state government help for sick and disabled | Set out fair wages and improved working conditions | Provided pensions for the elderly and widows | Replaced RA. Small farmers could get special loans to buy their land | Built camps for migrant labourers with decent living conditions |

New Deal legislation/agencies	Who was this aimed at helping?	Evidence	How would this help during the Depression?
Wagner Act			
Social Security Act			
Works Progress Administration (WPA)			
Resettlement Administration (RA)			
Farm Security Administration (FSA)			

• Opposition to the New Deal (pages 338–341)

3 Read the information and study the sources on pages 338–340 of your textbook then complete the tasks below.

   a Use the information in the text boxes to complete the diagram below on opposition to the New Deal. Add some extra details using page 338 of your textbook to help you.

Big business complained there were too many rules and regulations.	Huey Long's 'share the wealth' scheme wanted to reduce personal fortunes.	Dr Townsend campaigned for better pensions for the over-sixties.	Industry didn't like trade unions and said the market should sort wage levels.	Republicans said Roosevelt was too socialist/ communist.
The Republican Supreme Court declared some agencies unconstitutional.	Conservatives said the New Deal discouraged independence.	Father Coughlin attacked the New Deal for not doing enough.	Republican critics said Roosevelt was acting like a dictator.	Businesses complained of unfair competition from the TVA.

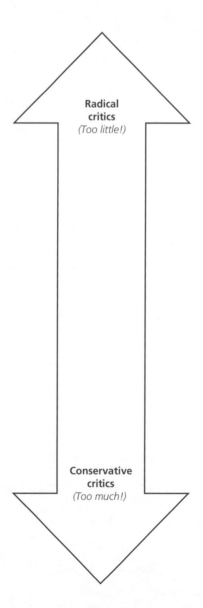

Radical critics
(Too little!)

Conservative critics
(Too much!)

b Create a brief profile of Huey Long in the space below.

Name: Huey Long

Political positions: ....

Policies: ....

....

....

....

Proposals: ....

....

....

c What tactics did Republican and business leaders use against Roosevelt?

....

....

....

d What evidence is there to suggest that most of the American population supported Roosevelt's New Deal?

....

....

e Why was the Supreme Court the most significant opponent for Roosevelt?

....

....

....

f   Give a brief explanation of why the Schechter Poultry Corporation Supreme Court appeal was such a blow to Roosevelt's New Deal reforms.

....

....

....

....

g   Choose one of the following cartoons: Source 11 on page 338, Source 13 on page 339, Sources 14 or 15 on page 340 or Source 17 on page 341. Explain how the cartoonist is trying to get their message across and which group/s would have sympathised with the cartoonist's message.

The cartoonist is trying to tell the audience that ....

....

The cartoonist does this by ....

....

....

I think that ....

would support this view. This is because I know that ....

....

....

4   Read the information and study the sources on pages 339–341 of your textbook then complete the tasks below.

a   How did Roosevelt respond to conservative opposition to the New Deal after 1936?

....

....

....

b What were the political and economic consequences of the 1937 budget cuts to the New Deal?

Political: ....

....

Economic: ....

....

c Which year was Roosevelt elected president for a third term? What does his re-election suggest about his popularity?

....

....

....

d What event caused many Americans to lose focus on the New Deal?

....

• The impact of the New Deal (pages 342–343)

5 Study the information on pages 342–343 of your textbook then complete the tasks below.

    a Find two pieces of evidence to complete the table below.

A new society	A divided society
1.	1.
2.	2.

b Study the section on industrial workers. Complete the mnemonic below to give at least three examples of how workers benefited from the New Deal and three examples of how business opposed these changes.

W ....

O ....

R ....

K ....

E ....

R ....

c Study Figure 16 (page 341) and the section on unemployment and the economy (page 342) then answer the following questions.

i List three ways in which the New Deal legislation helped lower unemployment levels during the Depression.

....

....

....

ii What caused unemployment levels to rise again after 1937?

....

iii What event finally solved the unemployment problem in the USA?

....

iv What other evidence is there that the economy was still not as strong as it was before the Wall Street Crash in 1929?

....

....

d Study the section on African Americans (page 343). Use the key provided to colour code the details of how far black Americans benefited from the New Deal legislation.

Benefit [ ]   **No benefit** [ ]

200,000 were employed by the CCC and other alphabet agencies.	They were still less likely to be given jobs.	Some got access to new housing projects.	Racial segregation was present in the CCC.
Mortgages were denied to black families in white areas.	No civil rights were introduced as part of the New Deal.	Lynching continued in the USA.	Some received relief as part of the New Deal.

e Study the section on women (page 343). Complete the diagram below to describe how far women were better off under the New Deal.

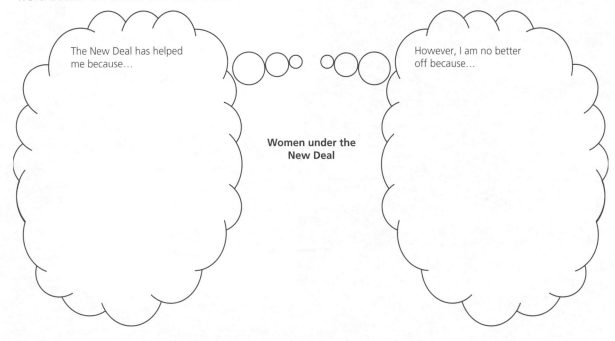

The New Deal has helped me because…

Women under the New Deal

However, I am no better off because…

f How far was the New Deal a success? Use the scales below to help you weigh up the evidence. Once you have listed all the winners and losers, decide which way the scales would tip. Use the space below the scales to explain, using evidence from your scales to support your judgements. (Remember, the most weighted side means more/stronger evidence!)

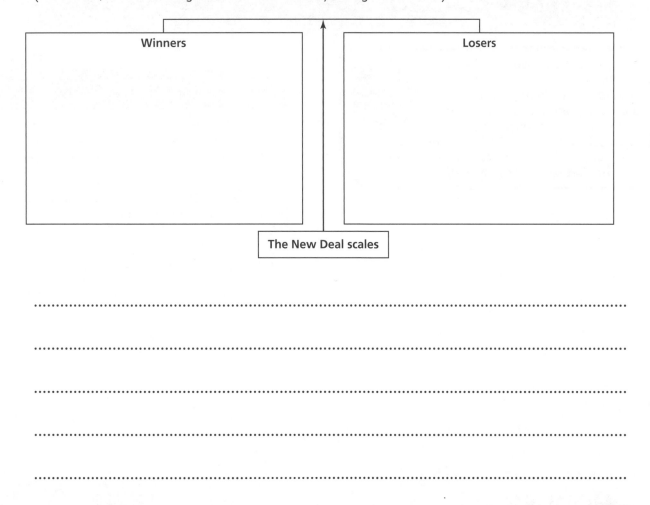

Winners

Losers

The New Deal scales

....

....

....

....

....

Reinforce learning and deepen understanding of the key concepts covered in the latest syllabus; an ideal course companion or homework book for use throughout the course.

» Develop and strengthen skills and knowledge with a wealth of additional exercises that perfectly supplement the Student's Book.

» Build confidence with extra practice for each lesson to ensure that a topic is thoroughly understood before moving on.

» Build a strong understanding of the main events of the course and the confidence to know how to use this knowledge.

» Keep track of students' work with ready-to-go write-in exercises.

» Save time with all answers available online in the Online Teacher's Guide.

Cambridge IGCSE™ and O Level

History
Option B:
The 20th Century
Second edition

Ben Walsh

DYNAMIC LEARNING   HODDER EDUCATION

Use with *ISCGE ™ and O Level History* 2nd edition
9781510421189

This resource is endorsed by
Cambridge Assessment International Education

✓ Provides learner support for Option B for the Cambridge IGCSE, IGCSE (9–1) and O Level syllabuses (0470/0977/2147) for examination from 2020.

✓ Has passed Cambridge International's rigorous quality-assurance process

✓ Developed by subject experts

✓ For Cambridge schools worldwide

HODDER EDUCATION
www.hoddereducation.com

ISBN 978-1-5104-4858-2

9 781510 448582

MIX
Paper from responsible sources
FSC™ C104740